Floral Motif
Volume 1
An Adult Coloring Book

A relaxing coloring book filled with repeating floral patterns to help you zone out, meditate, and relax.

By Victoria Clarke

Stay Calm and Color On!

Hey there!

Coloring has become an inexpensive and fun way to relieve stress and unwind after a busy day doing whatever it is you do!

Whether you work all day or take care of children or simply feel like the world is caving in, take some time to yourself and enjoy these floral designs. The repetitive patterns will help you get into the zone while your brain unwinds.

All of the art was designed with plant inspirations in mind so go wild with your colors and bring them back to life.

Enjoy ☺

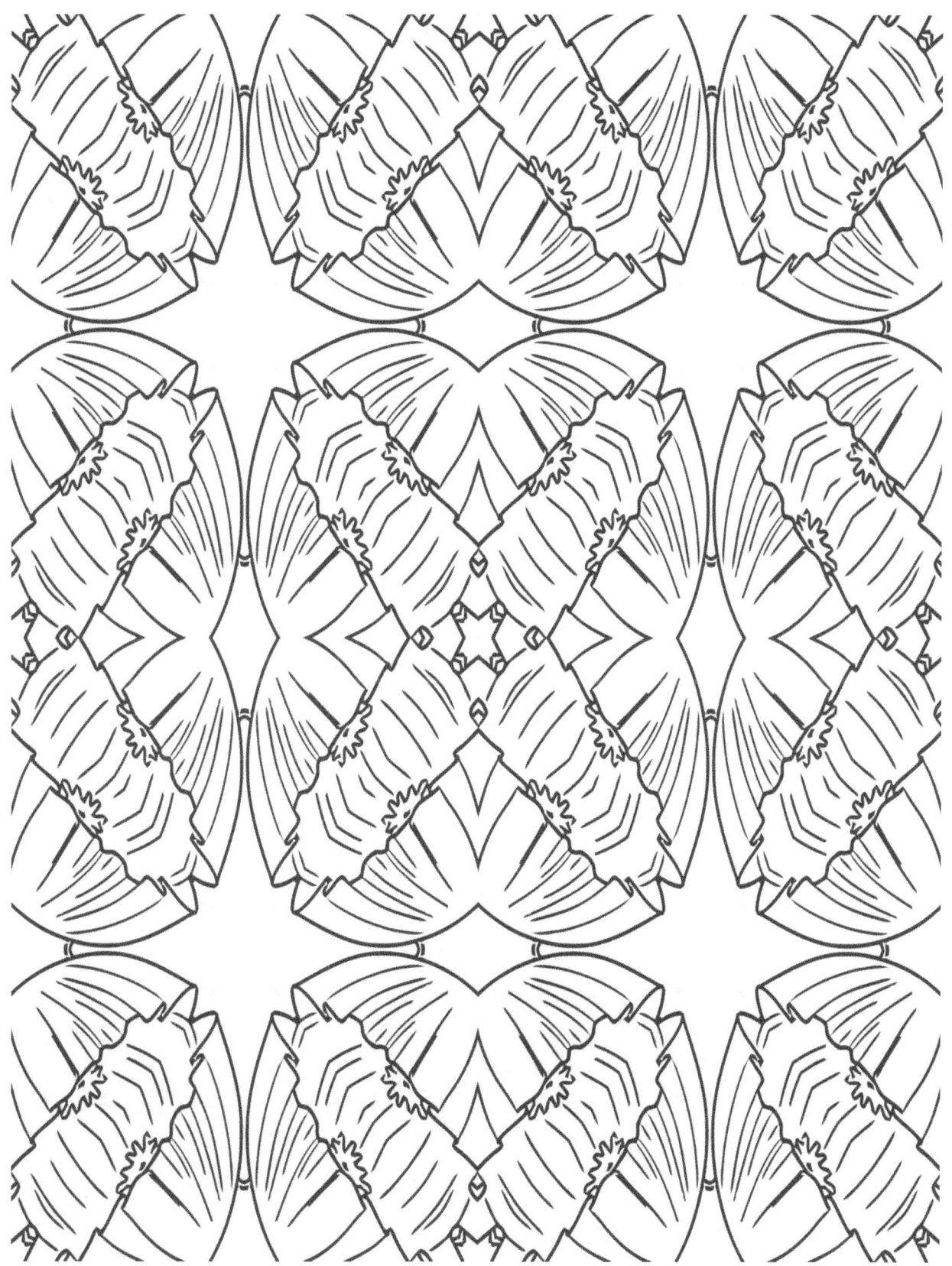

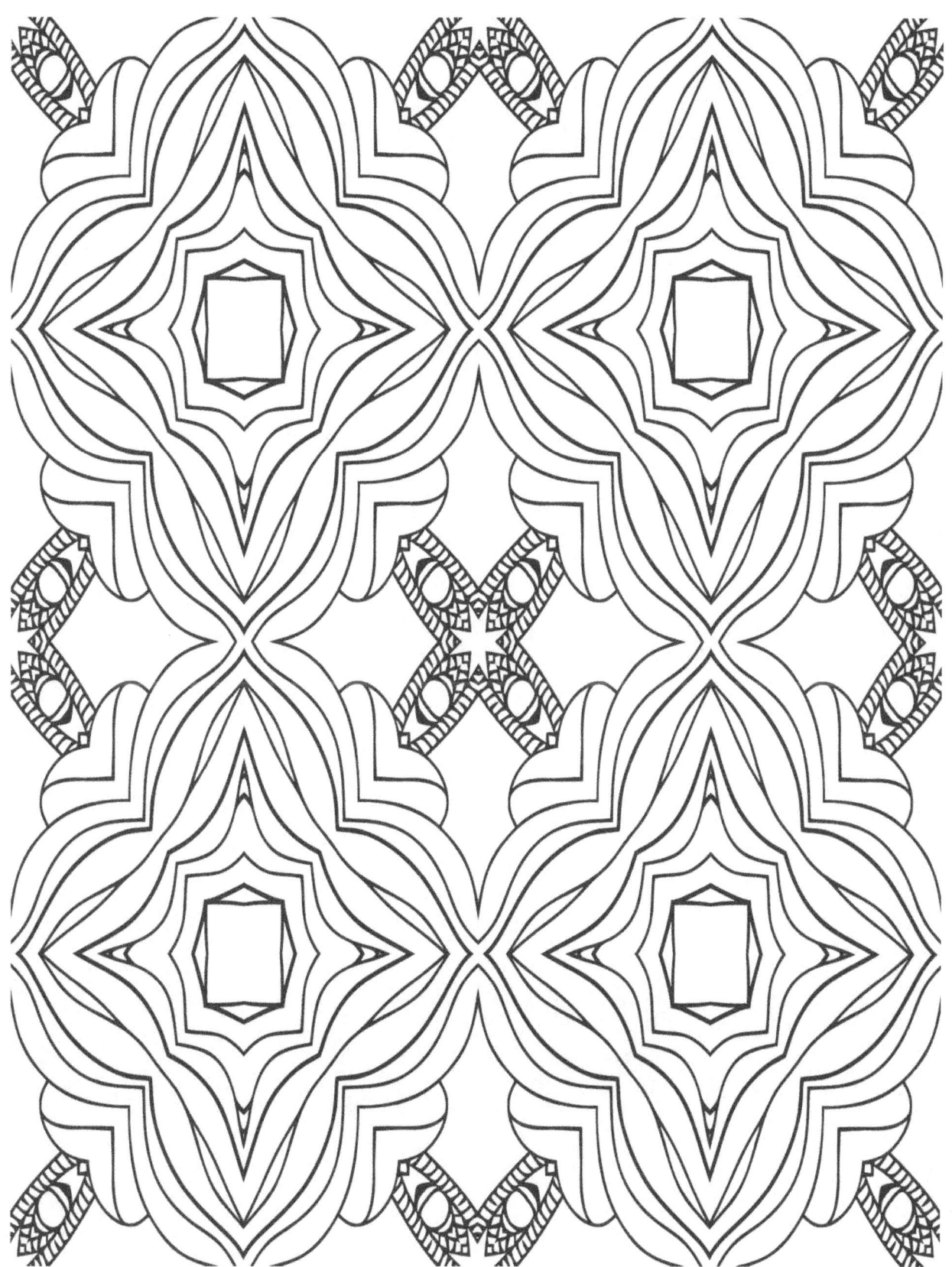

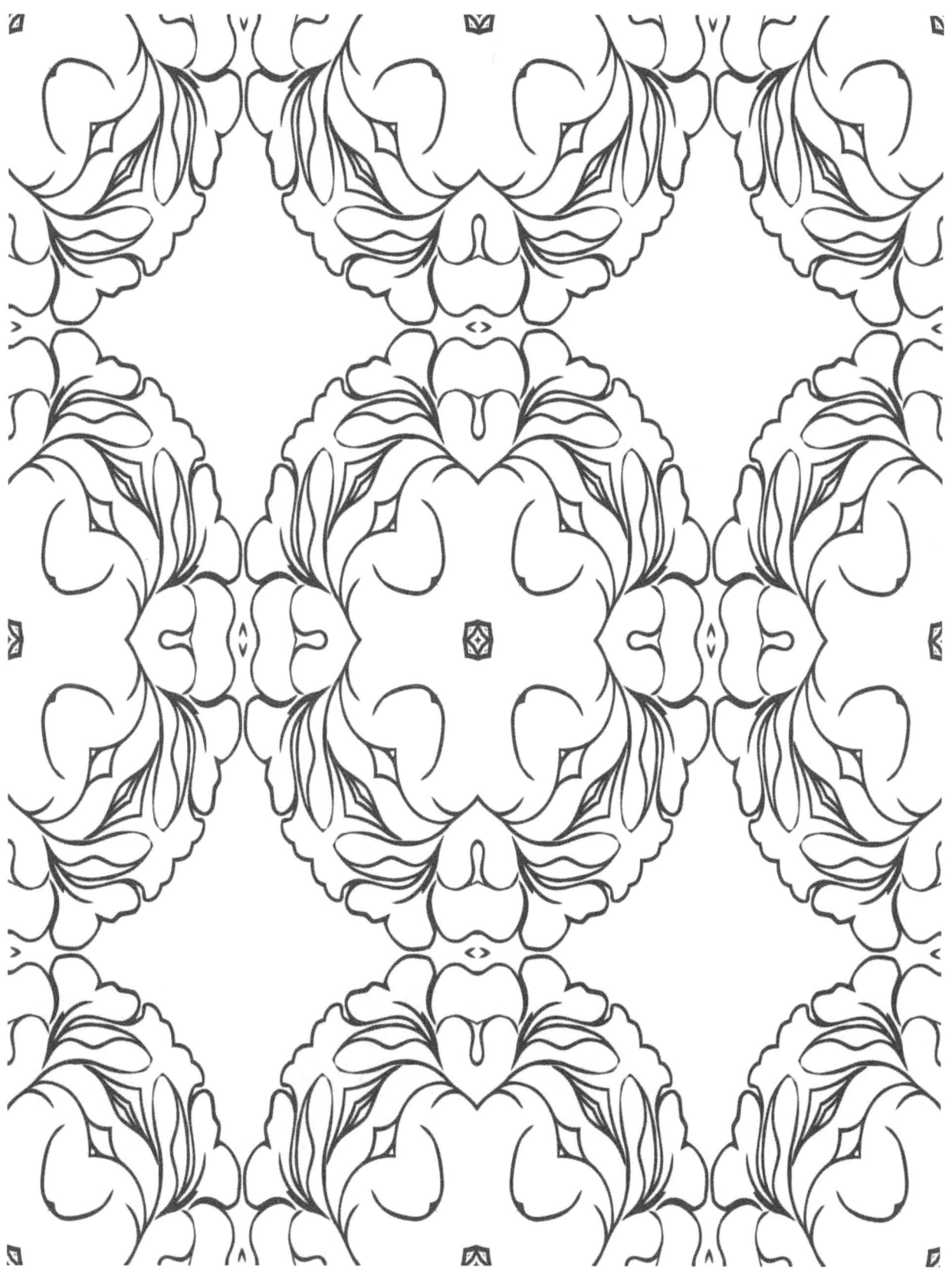

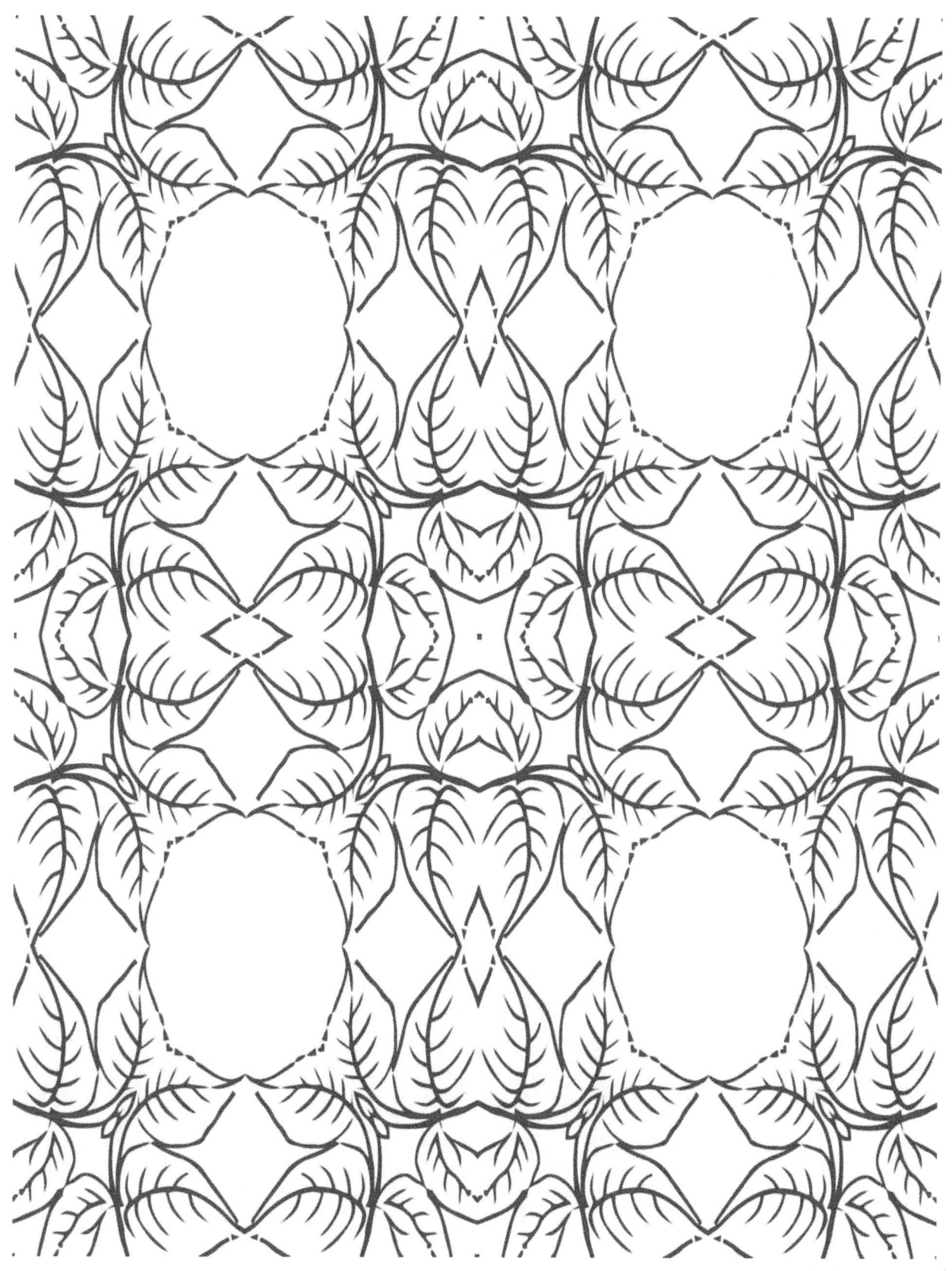

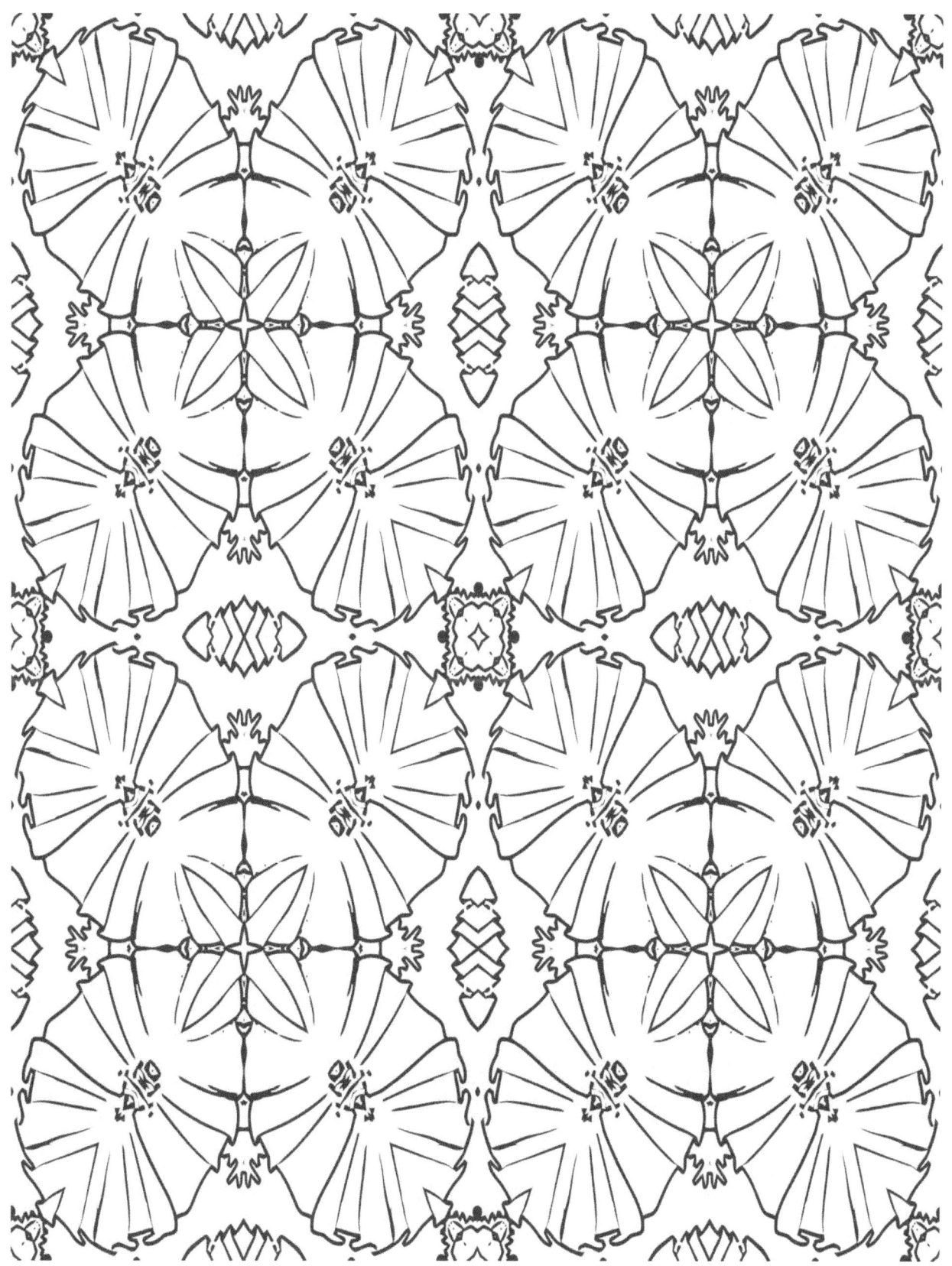

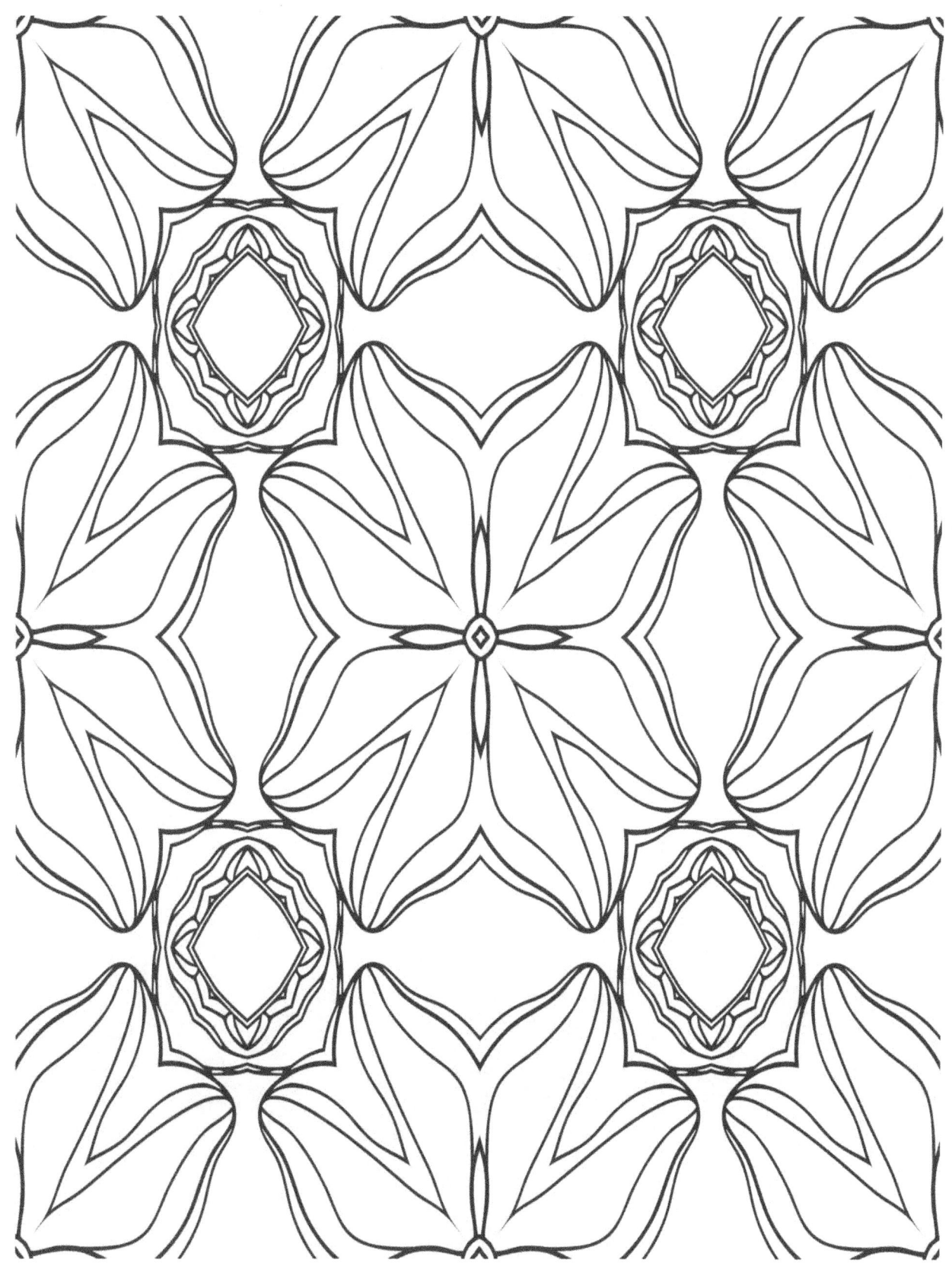

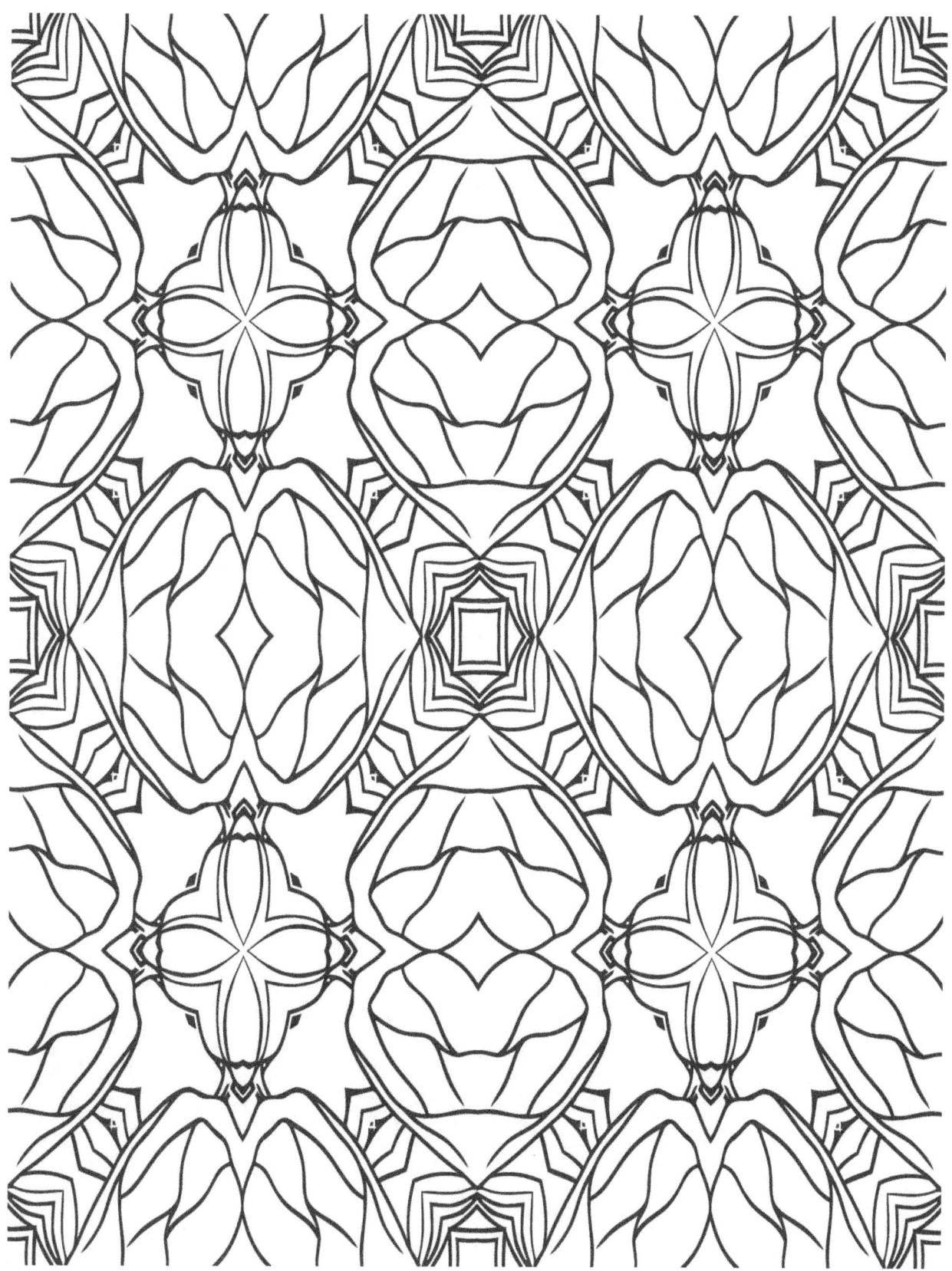

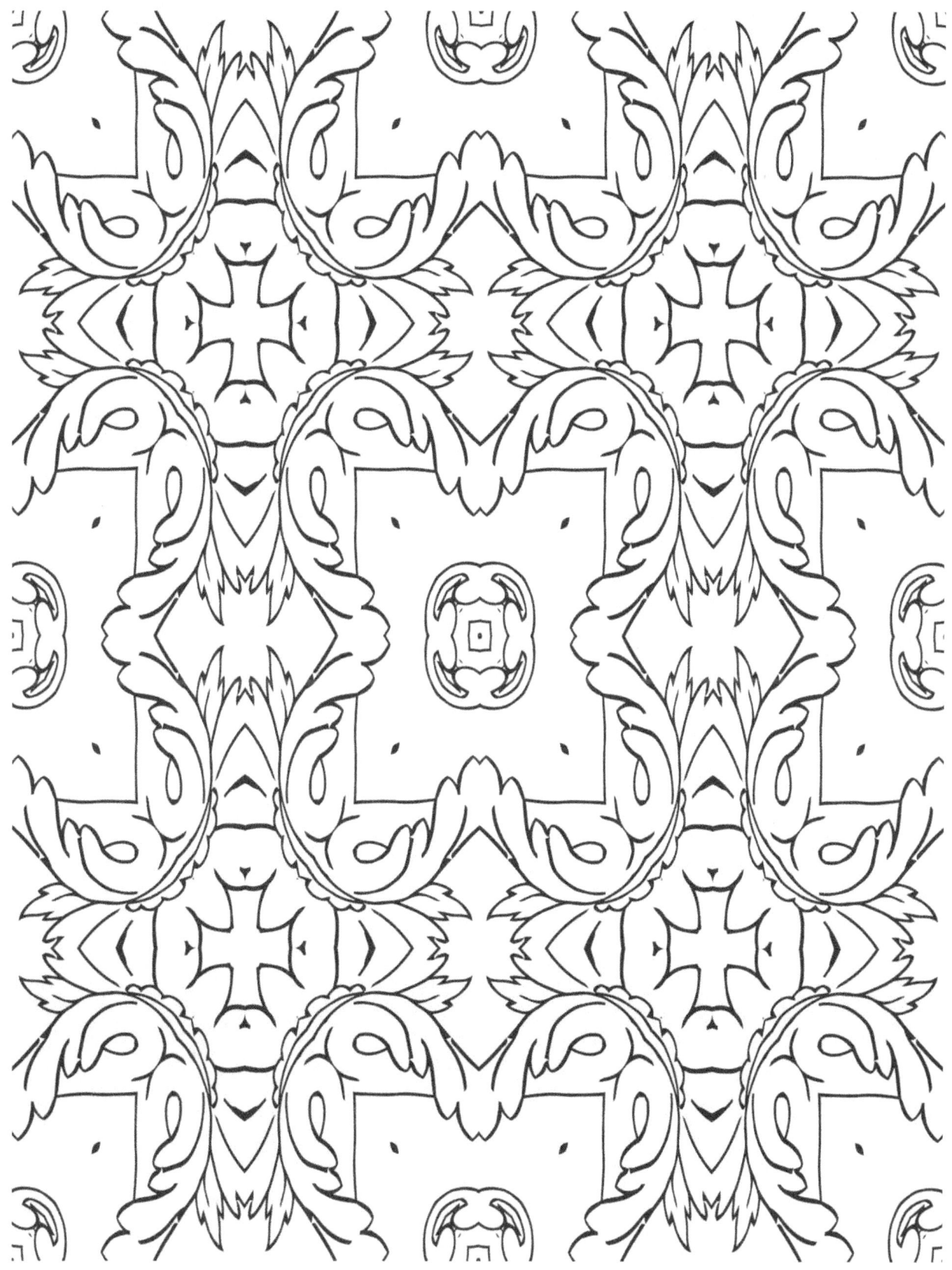

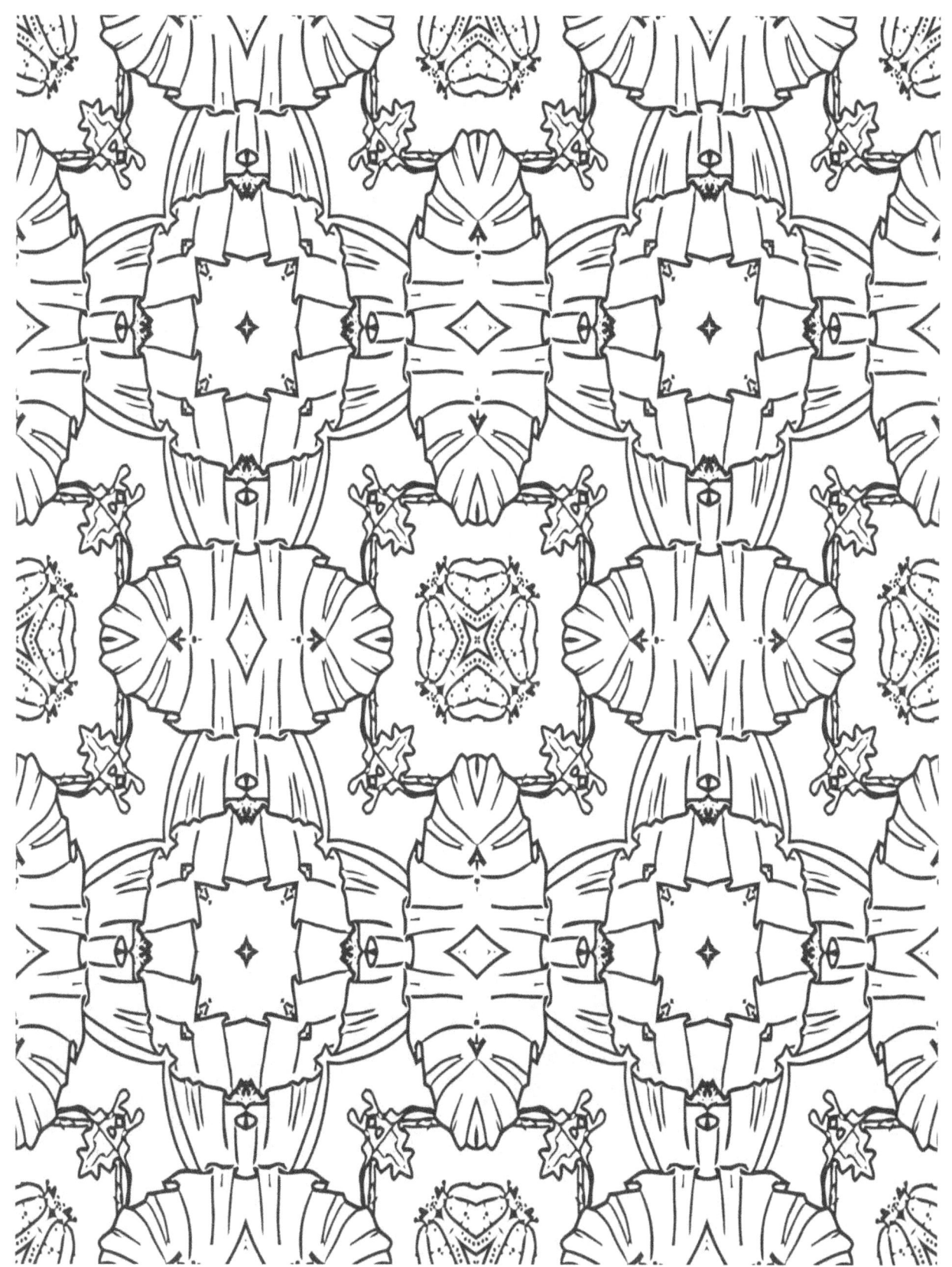

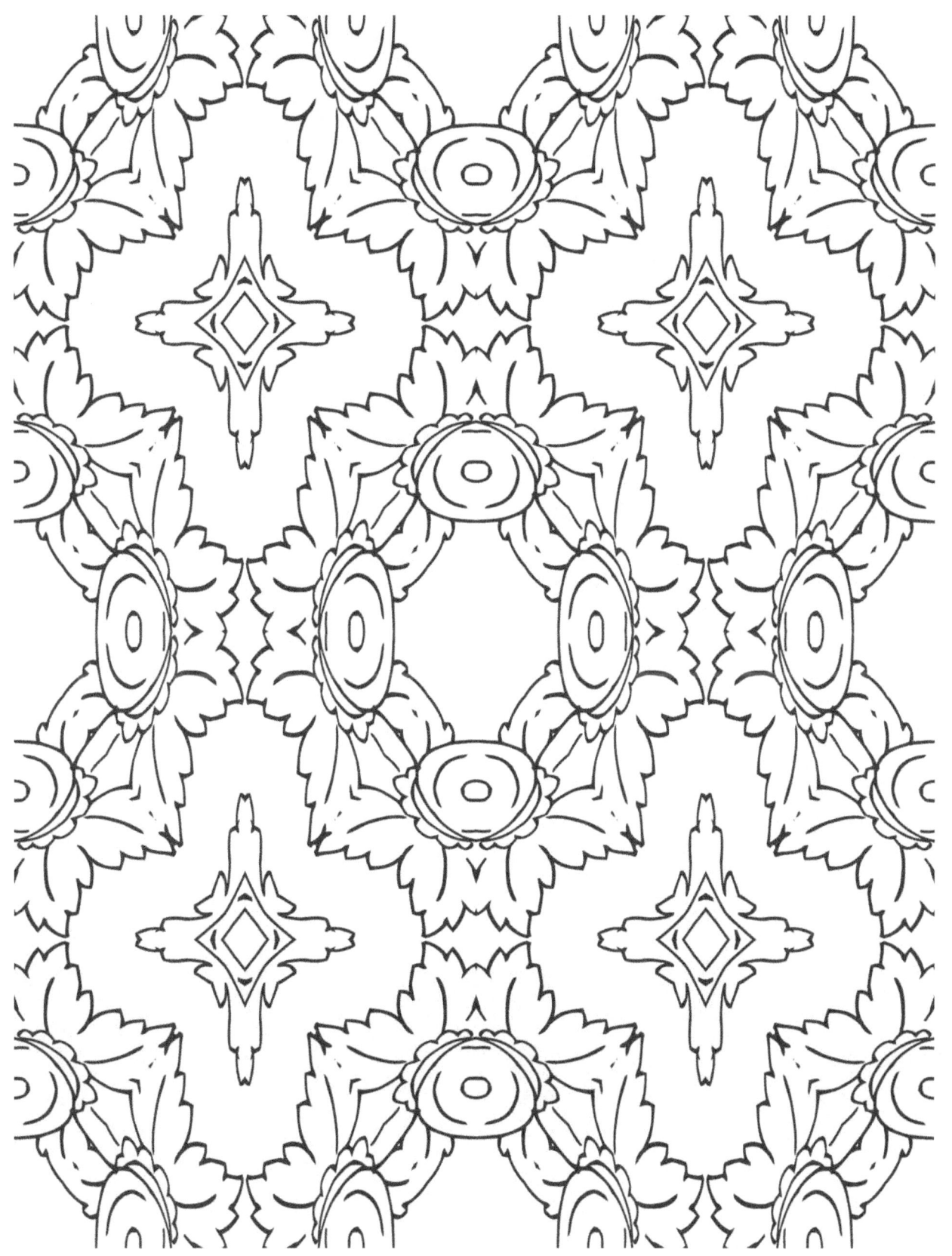

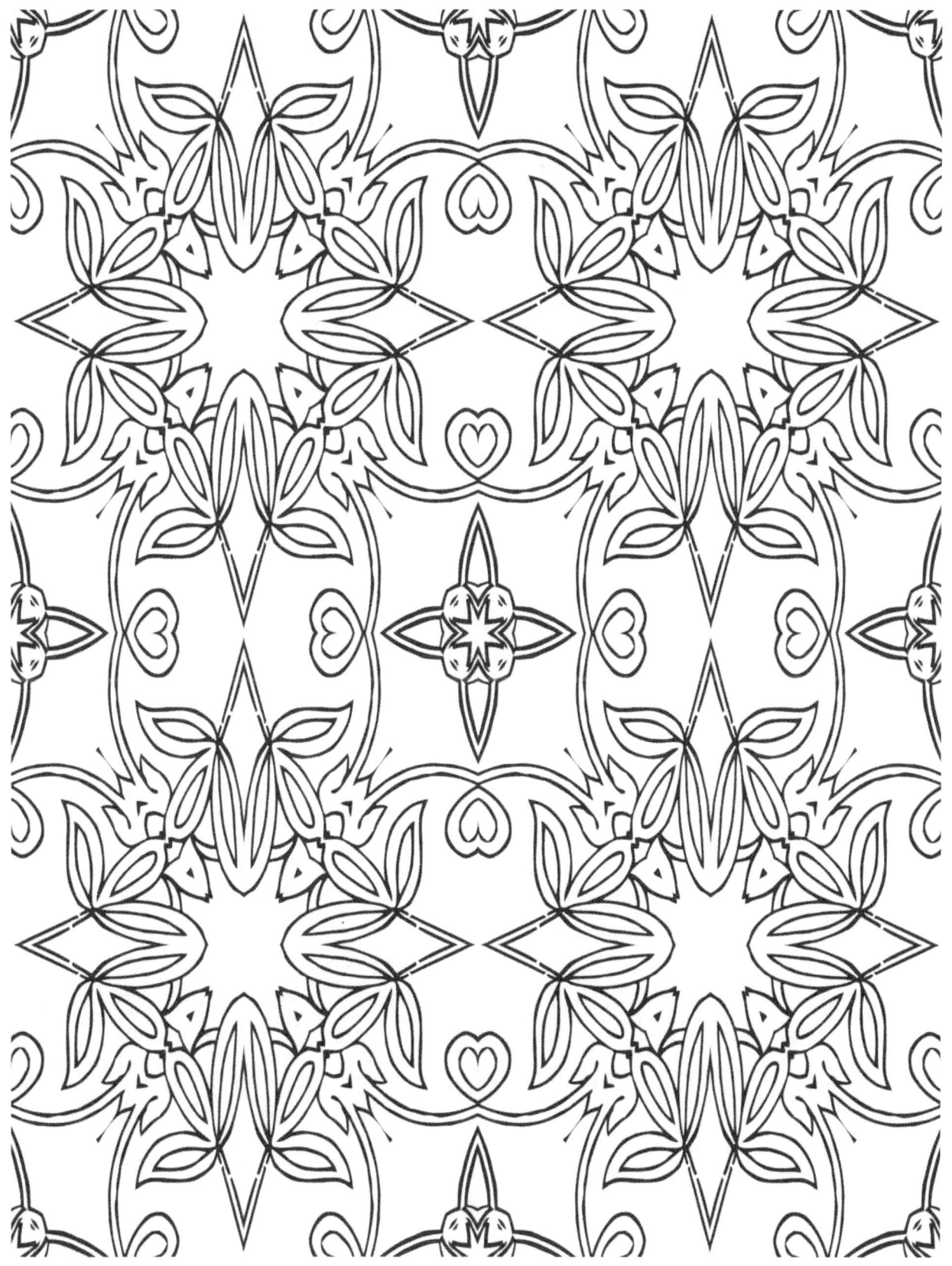

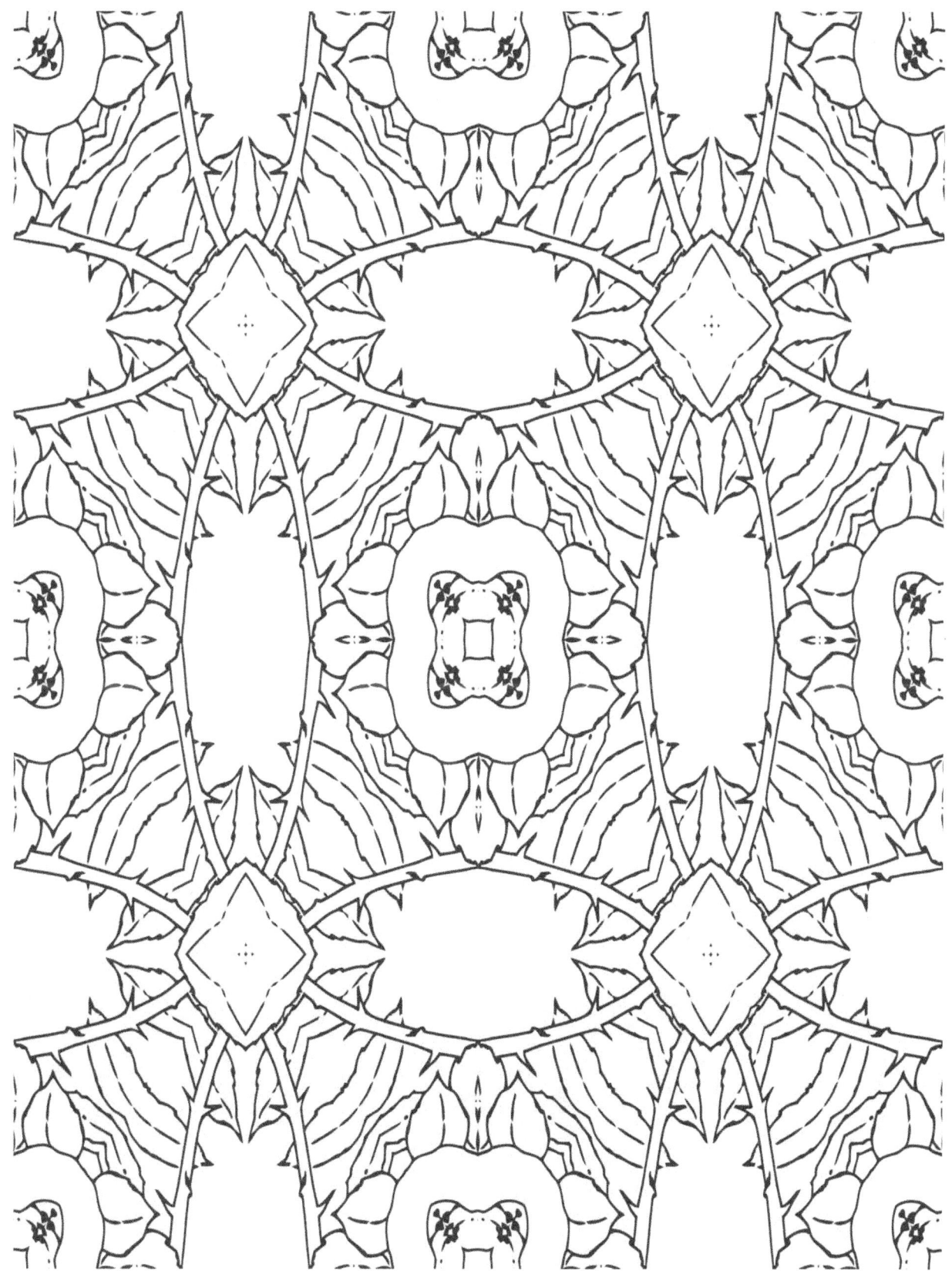

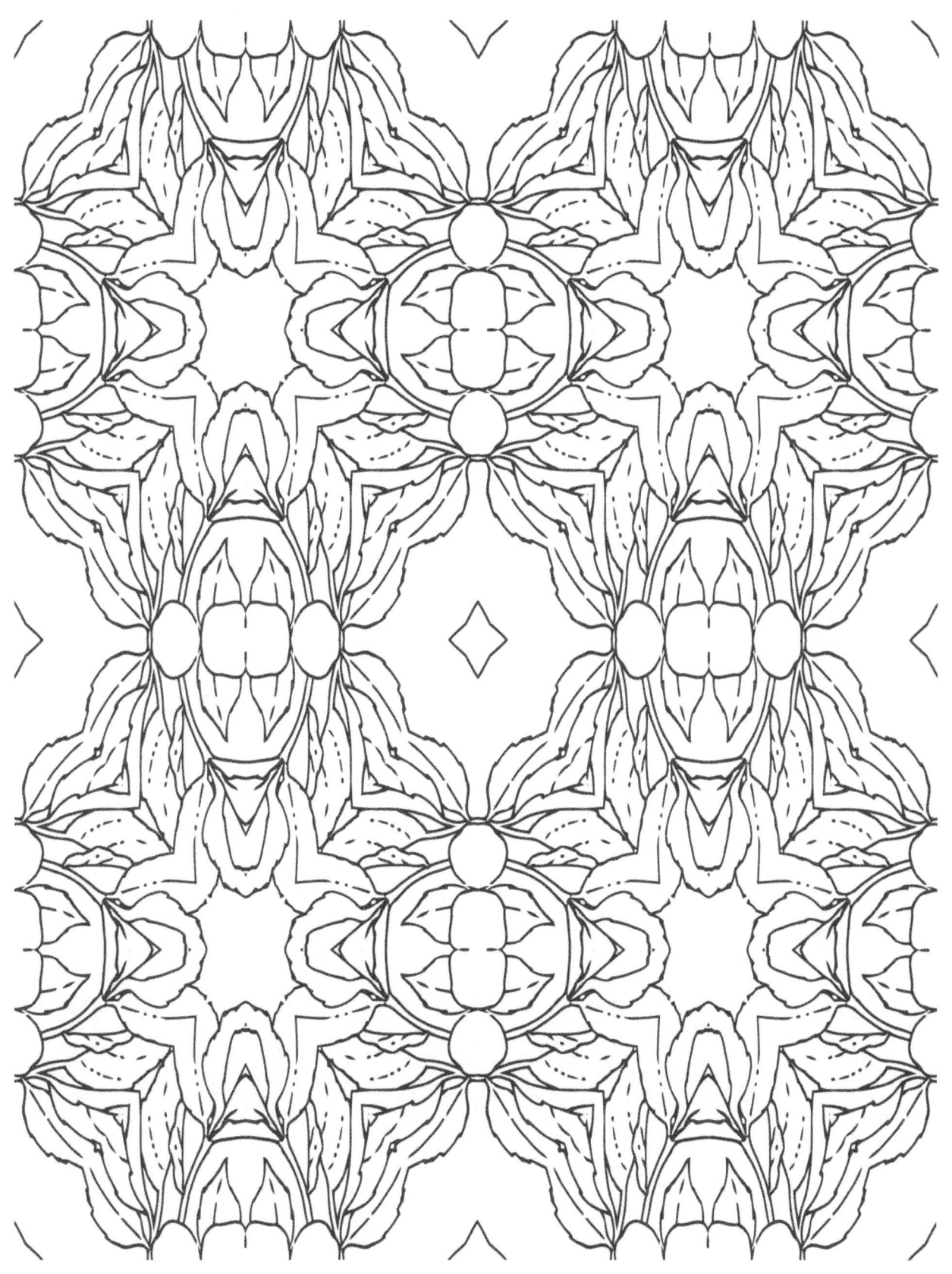

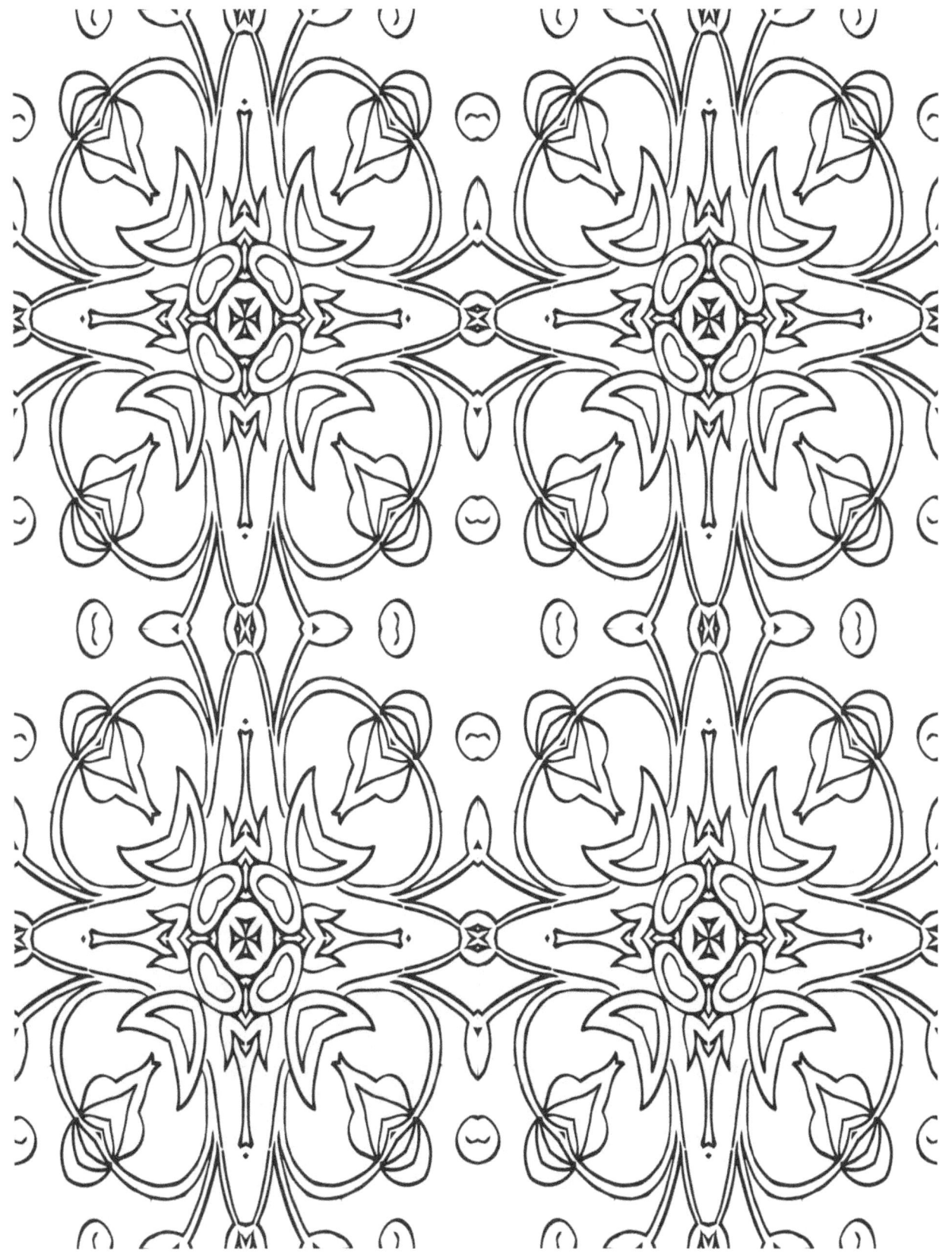

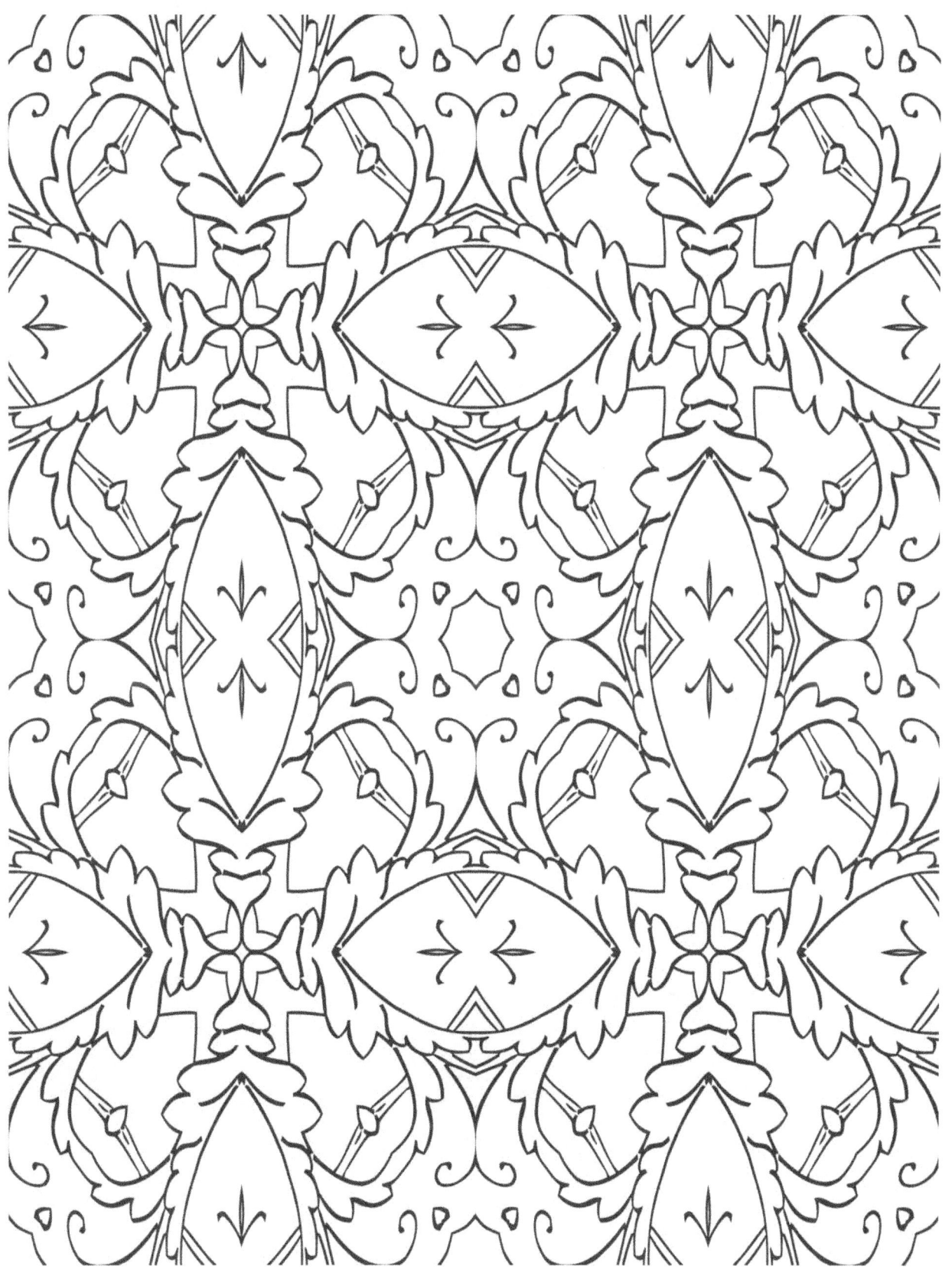

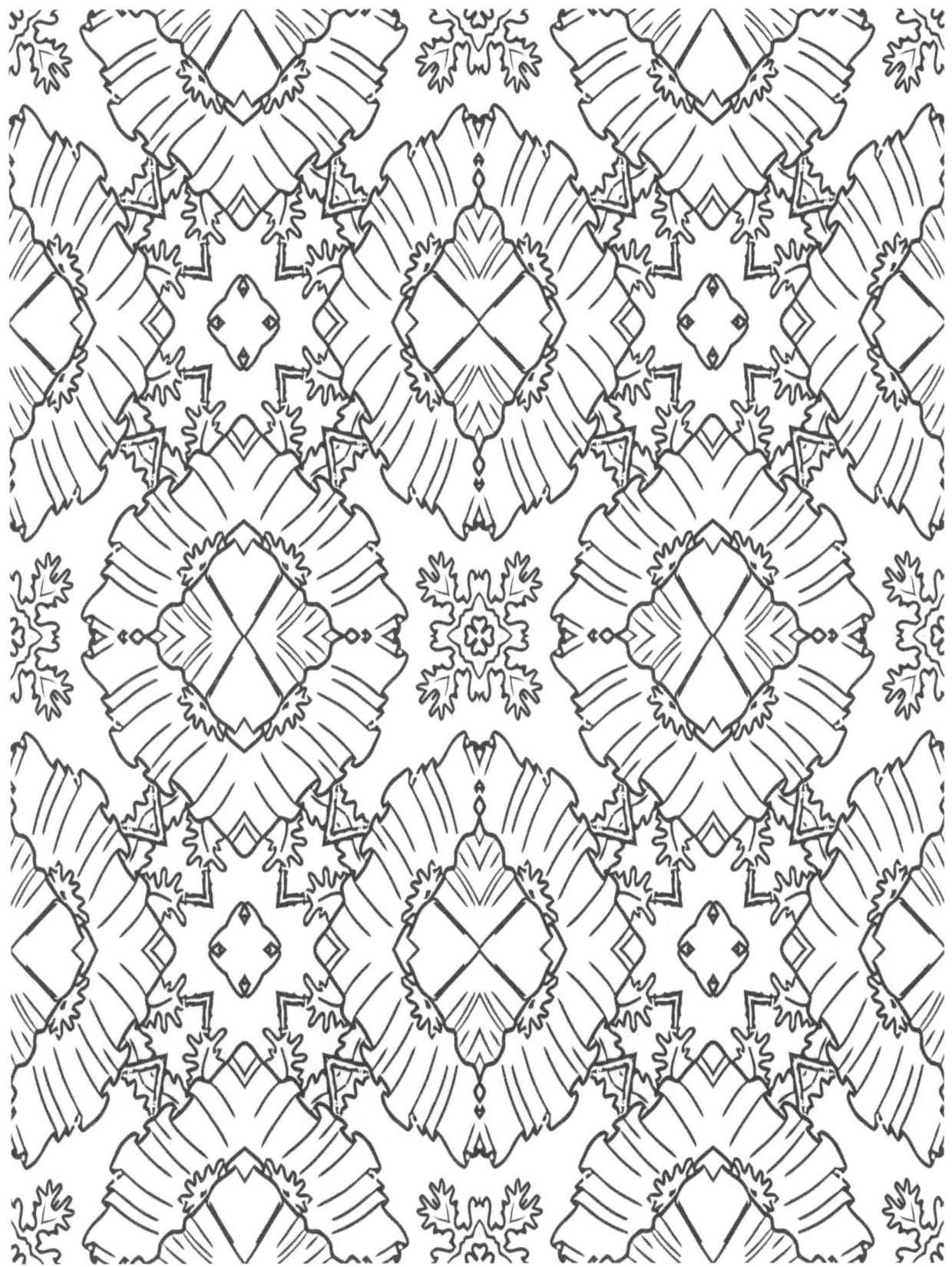

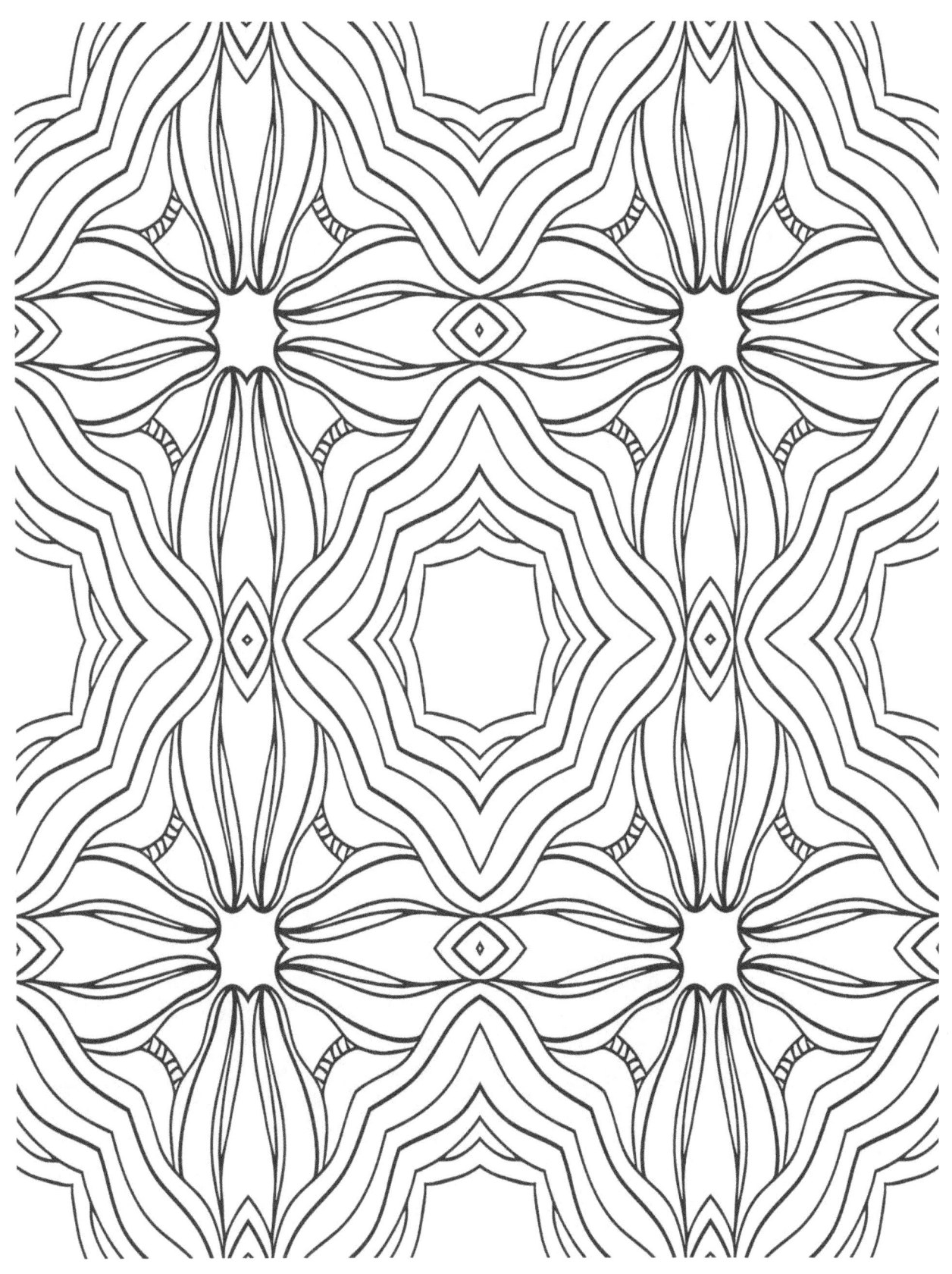

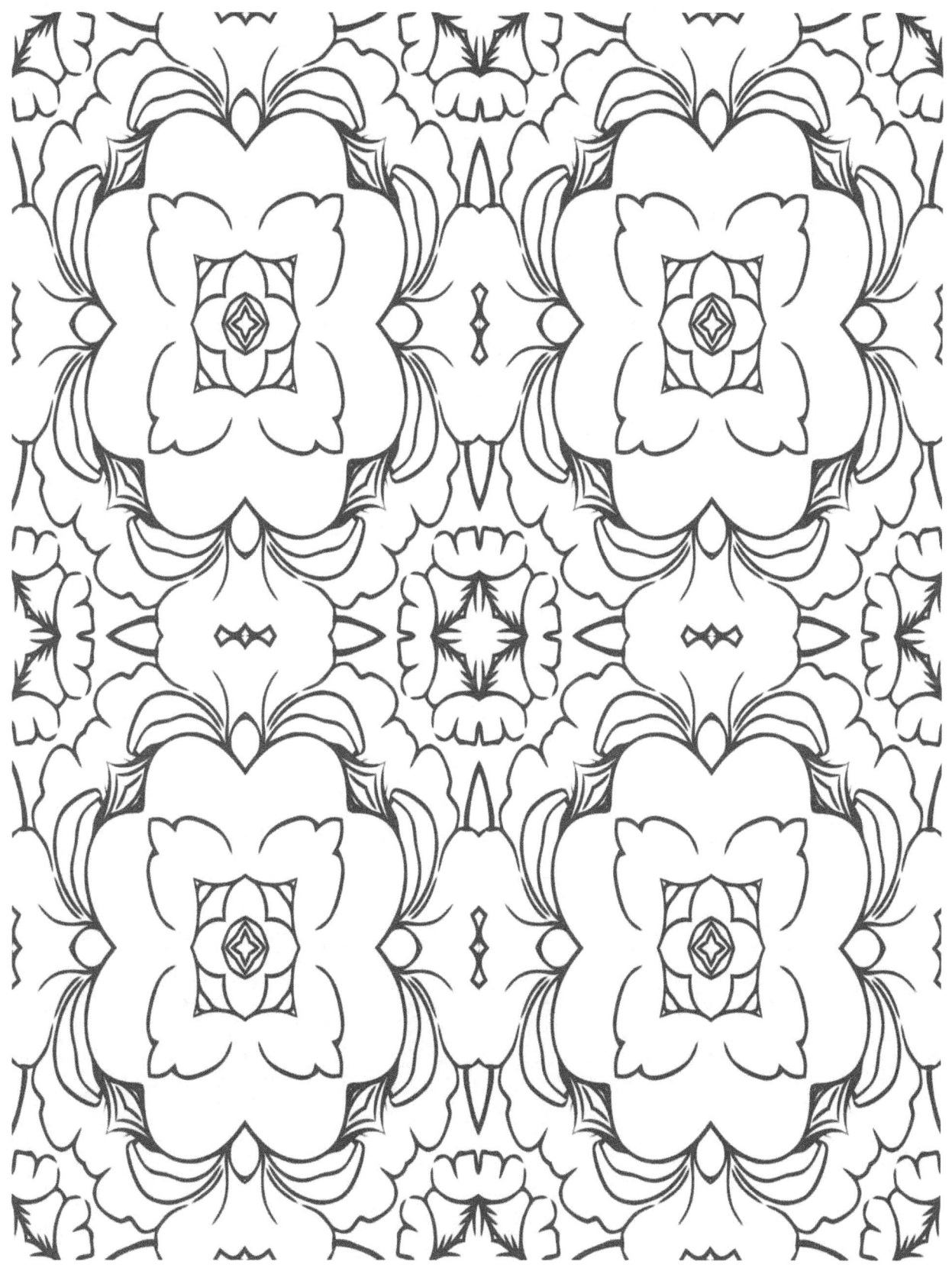

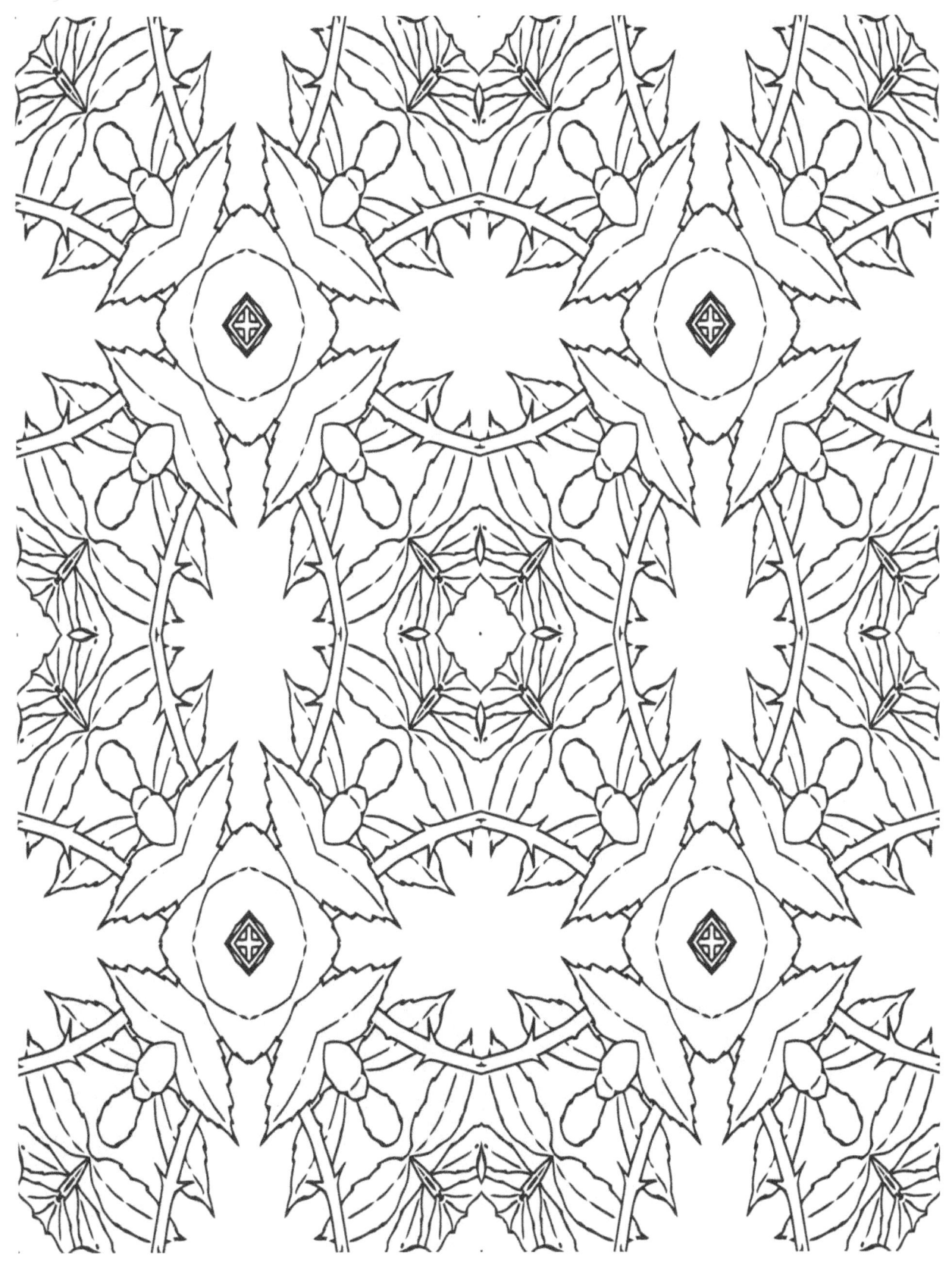

Please keep an eye out for new coloring books or visit **stressfreecoloring.org** for new options from me and info regarding other newly released coloring books!

If you enjoyed the coloring please let other color enthusiasts know by leaving a review ☺

Other Titles by Victoria Clarke

Yummy Treats – A Delicious Adult Coloring Book
25 Custom Illustrated Images of Treats

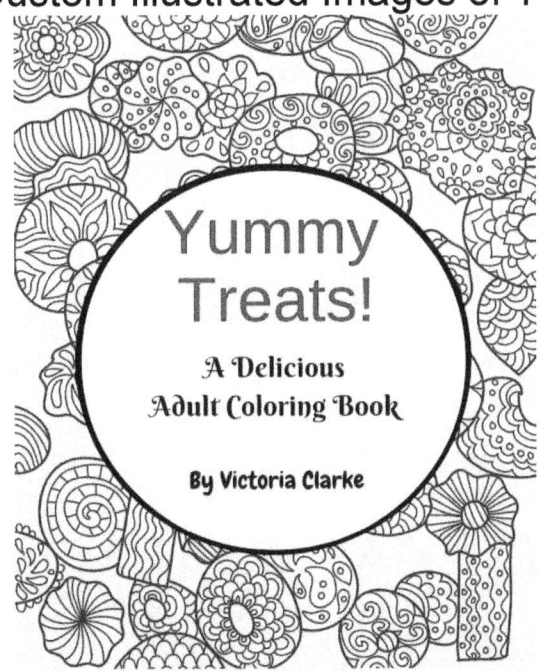

http://www.amazon.com/Yummy-Treats-Adult-Coloring-Book/dp/1532809301